LEFT FOR THE RISING SUN,

RIGHT FOR SWAN HUNTER

LEFT FOR THE RISING SUN,

RIGHT FOR SWAN HUNTER

THE PLEBS LEAGUE IN THE NORTH EAST OF ENGLAND 1908/1926

Robert Turnbull

Five Leaves Publications

Left for the Rising Sun,
Right for Swan Hunter
by Robert Turnbull

Published in 2014
by Five Leaves Publications
PO Box 8786, Nottingham NG1 9AW
www.fiveleaves.co.uk
www.fiveleavesbookshop.co.uk

ISBN: 978 19 10170076

Designed and typeset by
Four Sheets Design and Print

Printed by
Imprint Digital in Exeter

CONTENTS

ILLUSTRATIONS
PAGES 39–46

FOREWORD AND ACKNOWLEDGEMENTS

For the last two years I have been a researcher on the North East Labour History Mapping Popular Politics Project. This has been a two-year Heritage Lottery funded project, which aimed to uncover the often hidden history of the region. That research forms the basis of this book which, as far as I am aware, is the first in the region to explore the long neglected history of the Labour College movement in the North East of England.

Over several years of researching and writing on the Plebs League and the Labour College movement, I have accrued many debts in writing this book and would like to thank the staff at Hexham, Newcastle and Gateshead public libraries; The Working Class Movement Library in Salford; Ruskin College, Oxford; Northumberland Archives at Woodhorn and the staff at the Murray Collection; NEEMARC, University of Sunderland. I must also thank the staff at the Tyne and Wear Archives in Newcastle upon Tyne, the Lit'n'Phil, North East Institute of Mining, Modern Records Centre at Warwick University and Lawrence and Wishart

My special thanks to the following people: Dr John Charlton; Professor Sheila Rowbotham; Raymond King; Kate Bebby; Hannah Jones; Dr Joan Allen; Ross Bradshaw at Five Leaves Publications; Sean Creighton for the fantastic NEPP database; Dr Don Watson; Professor Willie

Thompson; Dr Tomaz Pierzochieck; Peter Nicklin; Dr Lewis Mates; Jennifer Kelly; Dr Richard Lewis; Dr Stewart Macintyre; Ben Sellers; Alex Gordon; Martin Levy; Margaret Levy; Mike Quille and, especially, Dave Tait for his wonderful comradeship. I must also thank the indefatigable Kevin Davies, whose continuing enthusiasm for the Good Old Cause is a source of inspiration to us all.

Thanks also to: Colin Waugh; Dr Geoff Walker; Tara Sutton; Keith Venables; Dave Chapple; Dave Harker; Dave Douglass; Jan Bownes; Helen Ford; Martin Saunders; the late Raphael Samuel; Dr Hilda Kean; the late Marian Sharples; Nicole Kroese; Lorna McGowan and the parents of 4M Sele First School Hexham. I would also like to thank Dr Keith Armstrong and Dr Hywel Francis for information on Noah Ablett. In the same vein I must credit Sian Williams and the staff at the South Wales Miners Library in Swansea for allowing me to view Noah Ablett's personal copies of *Plebs*. Thanks to the late Ivet Dixon for the wonderful memories, and for her deep knowledge of history and of Jamaica. I must also thank her husband Donald.

I also owe a debt to the Northern Shop Stewards Network and the various members of the Plebs League, both the original version and its twenty-first century equivalent who have proved to be a constant source of help and inspiration. Any interpretations and mistakes that remain are of course my responsibility.

It only remains for me to acknowledge the most important people — my family. Without their love and support, this book would never have seen the light of day, so my special thanks to my mum and dad Eric and Audrey Turnbull and to my three sons Christopher, Adam and Jake, and to Kim and the boys for putting up with me banging on about the revolutionary implications of the *Miners' Next Step*. This book is dedicated to Kim, Christopher, Jake and Adam with love and affection.

RT
June 2014

Introduction

In the last three decades there has been a revival of interest in the history of adult education and its subsequent
political implications. Following on from the pioneering
research of Stuart Macintyre some thirty years ago,[1]
Richard Lewis looked at the history of the Workers'
Educational Association (WEA), and its conflict with the
Plebs League in his book *Leaders and Teachers*[2], which
focused on South Wales and its revolutionary traditions.
In the same vein, the late Eddie and Ruth Frow explored
the history of what became known as autodidactism or
working class self-education, through their research in
Lancashire;[3] and much research has been done around
the influence of John Maclean and the Scottish Labour
College Movement.[4]

As far as I am aware, the only significant published
research into workers' education on Tyneside is *The Right
to Learn: the WEA in the North of England, 1910–2010*.
There have been small pieces of work on individual
aspects, most notably by Maureen Callcott who looked at
the struggle to establish a public library movement on
Tyneside in the 19th century. But it remains a mystery as
to why no-one has attempted to research the history of
working class education, and in particular the Plebs
League, in the North East of England. After all, Tyneside
was the cradle of the industrial revolution, and, along

with South Wales and Red Clydeside, it has an important place in the history and traditions of the British labour movement.

This book is therefore a contribution to our history, but it is more than that. I hope it is a reminder that education is a right and not a privilege, and that the struggle for liberty and equality must be renewed in each generation if the gains made by previous generations are to be built on and renewed. In the North East region, as in many others, we have seen libraries closed, the bedroom tax imposed on people, cuts to benefits, the disabled and unemployed scapegoated and vilified, in some of the most vindictive and cruel attacks by a ruling elite, certainly in my lifetime.

So how do we fight back? What lessons can we learn from the past that can aid us in our present struggle? What ideological tools can we use, and where is the tool kit? How do we begin that long march from what at times seems like servility, to a society which puts people before profit and which ensures that at least our kids have a decent start in life?

I want to suggest that the long march has to begin with an education that is rooted in the hopes and aspirations of working people, in much the same way that the founders of independent working class education argued over a hundred years ago. The one thing that the ruling class fears most of all is an educated, articulate working class which is able to meet it head-on and in the process take its arguments apart. Why, for example, is the general secretary of the Communist Party never invited onto the BBC's *Question Time*? Why indeed is the *Morning Star* never featured on the BBC press preview?

BACKGROUND TO THE PLEBS LEAGUE

What exactly was the Plebs League, and where does it fit into the long history of working class autodidactism in the North East? South Wales had, through the League, great orators such as Nye Bevan, the fine organic intellectual tradition exemplified by Noah Ablett and others, and *The Miners' Next Step*.[5] Who then were the Tyneside counterparts to the likes of Ablett, Arthur Horner, Will John Edwards and others?

If South Wales was the cradle of the Plebs League, then the North East of England can be described as its kindergarten. Many of the independent working class education activists in the North East Labour College movement went on to achieve national prominence in the labour and trade union movement or in other fields – most notably Will Lawther, Ebby Edwards and George Harvey in the mining industry, and the writer Harold Heslop, whose autobiography *Out of the Old Earth* is an essential read.[6] Sadly, many of the personalities that appear in my book are today little more than a footnote in history; but I hope that, in writing their story, I can bring the long neglected history of the North East Labour College movement to a new audience.

Ruskin College, which has played such a pivotal role in labour and trade union history, was once home to one of the most bitter and contentious disputes within the history of organised labour. The ramifications are still being felt to this day. For it was there, in Walton Street, Oxford (now part of Exeter College) during October 1908, that a group of students dissatisfied with not only the quality of Ruskin's teaching, but also its ethics, formed what became known as the League of the Plebs. Their stated aim was to "bring about a more satisfactory relationship between Ruskin and the wider labour movement" under the slogan, as they later suggested, of "Educate, agitate, organise".[7]

The Plebs League took its name from the writings of the American Marxist Daniel De Leon, whose book *Two Pages from Roman History*[8] had just been published by James Connolly's Socialist Labour Party (SLP). De Leon recalled the events of the first recorded general strike in history, the *secessio plebis* in 494 BCE in ancient Rome, when a group of plebeians or working class walked out of the city, in protest against their treatment by the wealthy patrician or governing class, and won a number of important concessions including the right to elect tribunes of the people, with power to veto the decrees of the Senate.

The parallels between ancient Rome and the founding of the Plebs League were obvious for a generation of working class intellectuals who had come to maturity at a time of huge economic, political, cultural, social and philosophical change. Contrary to popular belief, early 20th century capitalist society was in a state of flux. Underneath the veneer of Edwardian respectability new currents were emerging in the arts, literature and political philosophy, and these were to have a profound impact on the future shape and direction of Britain and the world. These included Cubism in art, the Georgian anthologies in poetry,[9] and the ideas of socialism as articulated by Marx, Engels, William Morris, H.M. Hyndman, Rosa Luxemburg, James Connolly, Tom Mann and others.

The simmering discontents which led to the Ruskin strike, and the growth of an emerging working class, in terms of political, cultural, social and economic power, found its expression in an educational philosophy, rooted in the materialist conception of history and class struggle, as advocated by Noah Ablett of the South Wales Miners' Federation, and others such as W.F. Hay, Will Mainwaring and Charlie Gibbons. Together they went on to write the famous syndicalist pamphlet, *The Miners' Next Step*.

In the North East that struggle was personified by men such as Will Lawther of Chopwell and George Harvey of Durham as well as Ebby Edwards of Ashington. In Scotland and especially Glasgow, it became synonymous with John Maclean, Harry McShane, Willie Gallagher and what became known as Red Clydeside.

12

The formation of the Plebs League in 1908, the sacking of the Ruskin principal Dennis Hird for his support for the students, and the bitter Ruskin College Strike of 1909, which eventually led the students to secede from Ruskin and set up their own Central Labour College (CLC), was a confrontation which shook the labour movement to its very foundations. The CLC, first in Oxford and later, until its closure in 1929 at Earls Court in central London, worked closely with the Plebs League, causing a split in the labour movement which has never really been resolved, between the reformist, social democratic, Fabian wing and those on the far left who advocated what has been termed 'education for revolution'.

The questions which the students at Ruskin were grappling with, and which they later published as a pamphlet entitled *The Burning Question of Education*, were these:

◆ What sort of education is suitable for the working class so as to enable working men and women to take their rightful place in the cultural, economic, political and social life of the nation?

◆ Is education a form of citizenship, a means of bridging the class divide, as the WEA and, a generation earlier, the university settlement movement had argued?

◆ Is education in the best traditions of Plato, a question that has always plagued Western civilisation?

◆ What is the good life? What is the good society? How do we achieve that good society?

◆ Is working class education to be provided for the workers by a small group of paternalistic, often university-educated lay people, or should the working class go it alone and establish their own educational initiatives free from the dominance of the universities and the ruling class?[10]

These questions were brought into sharp focus during 1908, by the publication of a report entitled, somewhat loftily, *Oxford and Working-Class Education*, advocating much closer links between Oxford University and Ruskin College. The Plebs League believed that that there was no future for the working class while their education remained in the hands of the wealthy and privileged, and so they began to formulate their own educational philosophy which became known as Independent Working Class Education, or IWCE. It was a philosophy which aimed at the emancipation of the working class by the people themselves, in much the same way that Marx and Engels had advocated some fifty years earlier. It was, as the late Professor Brian Simon once said, *"The Search for Enlightenment"*.[11]

In the first edition of its journal *Plebs* published in 1909, the League set out its vision. Noah Ablett, autodidact and a leading member of the Plebs League executive committee, argued:

"If the function of Ruskin College had been made quite clear, there could scarcely have been any dispute as to its policy. Everyone who is really anxious that the working class should raise itself to an independent and controlling position in this country will be confused on finding a 'Labour College' coquetting with the University …. They would naturally ask how an institution which has for centuries been the preserve of the aristocratic and governing classes could be of assistance to what is really an antagonistic movement."[12]

EDUCATION FOR BREAKING THE SERF STATUS

In his study of North East England, Norman McCord writes of the region that

"It was not an equal society, but it was not a society deeply riven with conflict, and that this is an important part of the background to the region's economic development, for such growth would have been much less likely in a society obsessed to any marked degree with revolutionary fervor or beset with a continual stream of political disturbances." [13]

14

How then do we explain a working class growing in political power and maturity in the years between 1900 and 1914? The North East's heavy dependence on coal, shipbuilding and heavy engineering bred a desire for self-improvement through learning and the Platonic ideal of the better life, which meant that the IWCE activists as well as the WEA were already pushing at an open door.

Writing in his autobiography, Jack Lawson recalled how he had been gripped by a belief that education was essential to "Breaking the serf status to which the manual worker is condemned." He continued:

> "We had great times and I was much encouraged. A group of us, including some school teachers, started an adult school with lectures and a gymnasium. There was also a very good art class. This went on for years in a building made by knocking two colliery houses into one. This, it must be reported, was long before the Workers' Educational Association or any such organisations had ever been heard of." [14]

The broadening of horizons often began through the local miners' lodge, continued through reading socialist literature such as Blatchford's *Clarion* and then went on through a career in local or national politics. Lawson recalled how, having joined the local branch of the Independent Labour Party (ILP), he began visiting a socialist bookseller in Newcastle on a Saturday, and began mixing with like-minded people from Northumberland and Durham. It was a road that led Lawson to study for a year at Ruskin College in 1907 and, ultimately, become an MP.[15]

At the same time as Lawson was on his way to Ruskin, his contemporary Ebby Edwards, a miner from Chevington near Morpeth, was beginning his journey on the same road. Unlike Lawson however, Edwards was to become pivotal in the dispute that led to the formation of the CLC, and was a leading figure alongside Will Lawther and George Harvey in the long struggle to establish the IWCE movement in the North East.

Social Tension and Industrial Unionism

For an organisation such as the Plebs League to develop, there had to be a large amount of social tension, a feeling that things could not go on as they were, and that a revolution was inevitable. After all, the founding members of the Plebs League were for the most part steeped in the language of classical Marxism and class war. To men such as Will Lawther and Noah Ablett, the idea of class collaboration was an alien concept. Ablett could not have put it better:

> "We want neither your crumbs nor your condescension, your guidance nor your glamour, your tuition nor your tradition. We have our own historic way to follow, our own salvation to achieve and by this sign we shall conquer."[16]

Perhaps more tellingly, George Harvey wrote:

> "The capitalist class is organised as a class with the necessary scientific groupings in such a manner that the whole body of the class can present a solid front able to act together as a whole, as well as in unit parts of the whole. The workers must be organised likewise, or be broken to the level of degraded wretches beyond redemption. Industrial unionism provides the basis of such organisation."[17]

So what was "industrial unionism", and how does this square with Norman McCord's earlier argument that the North East was essentially a settled society, without any of the social and political turmoil that affected the South Wales coalfield at this time? Harvey goes on to say:

> "Because of the fact that the industrial union is based on the war of interests between employers and workers, all workers in and about the mines join the Mining Industrial Union, without regard to nationality, trade or sex, recognising an injury to one as the concern of us all, and acting accordingly. This is certainly better than a federation with scores of unions, each with different leaders and different agreements .... This industrial form of

unionism renders it possible for us to strike a mine solidly from top to bottom, or if necessary the entire mining industry of Britain from end to end. If that will not suffice, we call on other industrial unions to assist us ... in order to defend or promote the interests of the workers."[18]

This is not a vision of a society at ease with itself, nor is it a vision of a society of enlightened, paternalistic employers in the Robert Owen mould. This is a recipe for class war and anarchy on a national scale.

OPTIMISM, COLLECTIVISM AND THE GREAT UNREST

George Harvey was born in the mining village of Beamish in County Durham on 7 August 1885. Four years older than Will Lawther, and some two years younger than Noah Ablett, he was an early member of the ILP, which had been formed in order to bring about working class representation in Parliament, without having to do deals with the Liberals and other factions. Dave Douglass is correct when he suggests that the ILP was then "more of a movement or platform to which all wings of the working class political movement could affiliate."[19]

The problem was that there were almost too many factions to choose from. As well as the Independent Labour Party, there was the Socialist Labour Party (SLP) headed by James Connolly, the Social Democratic Federation (SDF) led by Hyndman, and the new doctrines of syndicalism and industrial unionism, as articulated by Noah Ablett, Tom Mann and others. There was also the aforementioned *Clarion* newspaper edited by the ex-soldier Robert Blatchford, selling some 90,000 copies per week at the end of the 19th century.[20]

It was a time of massive optimism within the ranks of the socialist movement, with new groups and methods of thinking appearing all the time. Geoff Walker notes that, in February 1908, the SLP managed to gain a foothold in the North East for the first time, when James Macmurran of the Newcastle Socialist Society requested details and application forms for a possible branch in Newcastle. Later that year a meeting was held in Wallsend attended by over 400 people where a lecture was given on 'Industrial Unionism'. Prior to this the region had been an ILP stronghold.[21]

In the year that George Harvey spent at Oxford, the SLP on Tyneside seems to have grown massively, with branches established in Wallsend and Gateshead. Walker goes on to say that by October 1908 the Gateshead branch of the SLP was holding regular meetings on a Saturday morning, producing its own propaganda. As a result of these meetings the SLP seems to have entered into debates with the SDF as well as the ILP.[22]

The Plebs League can be said to have originated in the activities of organisations like the SLP and the propaganda efforts of men like Ablett, and women such as Mary Bridges Adams. A strong political focus required a sufficient body of theoretical knowledge, to enable people to withstand the counter-arguments that invariably accompanied any discussion of what a socialist society might look like in the future. The Plebs League itself said:

"Education is and must always be a means to an end. To some it is a means to personal satisfaction, to others a means to a living; to us it is a means to the Great End, the emancipation of the workers. What above all else we need to know is the nature and source of the social forces pointing towards that end and the quantity and quality of the obstacles likely to arise. Thus social forces, their nature, origin and end constitute the general subject of our studies."[23]

This was the environment in which George Harvey, Will Lawther, Ebby Edwards and others grew up. Their political outlook had been forged by the common bonds of community and a socialist gospel which stressed collectivism and social solidarity among the working class so as that they might achieve the new society of which they dreamt.

The period 1910 to 1914 has been referred to by liberal historians as the 'Great Unrest'. It was an era of unparalleled industrial militancy, featuring miners, dockers, railway workers, the suffragettes, and those demanding Irish Home Rule. There were the shootings at Llanelli,[10] the Cambrian Combine strike, the so-called 'Tonypandy Riots' and *The Miners' Next Step*. It was the period of gunboats sailing up the Mersey, and of the Dublin Lockout of 1913.

In all of these disturbances the advocates of IWCE played a role, for central to the notion of industrial struggle was that of theoretical education and its relevance to everyday life, and their belief that nothing good could come out of education while it remained solidly in the hands of the ruling class. An editorial in the first edition of *Plebs* was emphatic:

> "If the education of the workers is to square with the ultimate object of the workers – social emancipation – then it is necessary that the control of such educational institutions must be in the hands of the workers. Beware of the sounding brass and the tinkling cymbal of ruling class-professed sympathies with labour."[24]

FOUNDATION OF THE NEWCASTLE LABOUR COLLEGE

How the new society was to be achieved, when in many instances the working class appeared – on the surface, at least – to be happy with the status quo, is a question that appears not to have troubled the founders of the CLC in the North East. Writing in *Plebs* in 1915 one G. Caruthers suggested:

> "It is a stiff and uphill struggle here as all the prosperous institutions and popular personalities support the WEA

method; yet we live in hope, knowing that, by our perse-
verance, the claims of our cause will win the support they
deserve."[25]

His optimism was well founded, for a year earlier in July
1914 *Plebs* had carried a report of a meeting at which the
Ashington Miners' Lodge had put forward a resolution to
withdraw the Northumberland Miners' Association scholarships from Ruskin College and transfer them to the
newly formed CLC. In a lengthy report in *Plebs* the arguments and counter arguments were rehearsed. The main
charge put forward by the advocates of the CLC seems to
have been the inadequate time to prepare their case; and
it was this, together with the falsehoods by the advocates
of Ruskin, which meant that the resolution was defeated
by 42 votes to 21.[26]

The report ended on a note of optimism but bemoaned
the fact that the Northumberland miners had not been suf-
ficiently politically developed to make a distinction between
the sort of education being offered by the CLC and that at
Ruskin. The debate was a harbinger of things to come, and
over the next several years the North East Labour College
movement grew and matured until it rivalled that of South
Wales in its scope and development.

Much of this was due to the work of George Harvey,
Ebby Edwards of the Northumberland Miners and Will
Lawther of Chopwell, all of whom became active in the
North East Labour College movement. Lawther was born
on 20 May 1889 at Choppington in Northumberland, of
impeccable dissenting heritage, his grandfather having
served time in prison for Chartist activities. He was the
seventh son of Edward Lawther and Catherine Phillips,
and the first to survive childhood. There were fifteen children of the marriage; and Lewis Mates in his study of
Lawther suggests that as a result Will was forced to grow
up fast.[27]

Like his contemporary Ebby Edwards, Lawther
attended Ruskin College, where he was tutored by Noah

Ablett, whose influence on his political development was such that Lawther later referred to him as "the greatest prewar Marxist".[28] On his return to the North East Lawther quickly established himself as an able propagandist, both in his local miners' lodge of Chopwell and also within the burgeoning IWCE movement nationally. It was an organisation and a philosophy that was well suited to Lawther's ability at this time, for it was through the efforts not only of Lawther but of other propagandists that the doctrines of syndicalism began to take hold among the working class.

So, given that the groundwork appeared to have been laid, it is surprising that the IWCE movement took a long time to get off the ground in the North East. It is interesting that Lawther was in touch with leading Welsh militants of the day and that he was very active in selling *The Miners' Next Step* in the Durham Coalfield. Bob Holton in his study of British syndicalism suggests that by this stage Lawther was moving towards anarcho-syndicalism.[29] There are also numerous examples in *Plebs* around 1914–1915 of Ebby Edwards lecturing for free in the Ashington area, on industrial history and other subjects. But it was not until 14 October 1916 that the Newcastle and District Labour College was formed.[30]

At the inaugural meeting, in Pilgrim Street, Newcastle, Will Lawther and George Harvey were announced as founder tutors, and sixteen members were enrolled for the class on economics and the modern working class movement. Lawther had appealed through the pages of *Plebs* for as many Durham miners as possible to join.[31] At this point the Durham Miners' Association (DMA) supported the WEA.

One of the features of the early years of the IWCE movement in the region was the hostility between the advocates of IWCE and the WEA. In 1917 *Plebs* published a long article as a reply to Mr Mactavish of the WEA as they argued the merits of their respective educational philosophies. It is summed up in their article as "The WEA educates, The Plebs League merely instructs". [32]

From around 1917 onwards the IWCE movement in the area began to take off. It is clear from the reports of conferences and the number of classes that there was a hunger for education. For example, the 1925 annual report stated that the number of classes had increased to forty-four with a "pleasing increase" in the number of women. An indication of the success of the IWCE movement can be seen in the comment that "The capitalist press has not yet praised our work but is extremely alarmed at our growth."[33]

It is indicative of the long struggle, not to say drive, of the likes of Edwards, Harvey and Lawther that the North East was able to have an IWCE movement at all. Some of the autodidacts who made up the North East Labour College movement are long forgotten, but the energy, drive and determination of these people was quite remarkable. This is their story.

FOOTNOTES

[1] See Macintyre, S. *A Proletarian Science: Marxism in Britain 1917-1933* (Cambridge University Press, 1980) and Macintyre *Little Moscows: Communism and Working Class Militancy in Inter War Britain* (Croom Helm, London, 1980)

[2] Lewis, R. *Leaders and Teachers. Adult Education and the Challenge of Labour in South Wales 1906–1940.* (University of Wales Press, Cardiff, 1993)

[3] The best place to start is the Working Class Movement Library in Salford and in particular Ruth and Eddie Frow's account of radical Manchester entitled *Manchester: Working Class History Walk* (1983) in which they discuss the Labour College movement as well as the birth of the *Clarion* newspaper.

[4] See Duncan, R. and McIvor, A., eds. *Militant Workers: Labour and Class Conflict on the Clyde 1900–1950. Essays in honour of Harry McShane* (John Donald, Edinburgh, 1992) and in particular the article by Duncan 'Independent Working Class Education and the formation of the Labour College Movement

in Glasgow and the West of Scotland 1915-1922'. For the struggle to establish a public library movement on Tyneside, see Callcott, M. 'Libraries for the Working Class in 19c Newcastle' (*North East History Journal* 2004 pp.99–111).

[5] Ablett, Gibbons, Gill, Rees et al *The Miners' Next Step* was a pamphlet published in 1912 which called for coalminers through their lodges to embrace syndicalism and a new "scientific trade unionism. The main author is recognised as being Noah Ablett although this was very much a collaborative venture.

[6] Heslop, H. *Out of the Old Earth* (Bloodaxe Books, Newcastle Upon Tyne, 1994). Harold Heslop was a miner who attended the Central Labour College in the 1920s. He later became a writer and was honoured by the Soviet Union. This book is his autobiography.

[7] Ablett, Sims et al *The Burning Question of Education* (Plebs League, Oxford, 1909) p.3

[8] De Leon, D. *Two Pages from Roman History* (Nabu Press, South Carolina, 2010).

[9] The Georgians were a group of poets who were active in the years immediately before WW1. They were interested in nature, and the countryside and wanted to imagine England as a pre-industrial rural idyll. Their number included Rupert Brooke, Wilfrid Gibson and Edward Thomas.

[10] *The Burning Question of Education op cit* and especially pp.4–10

[11] Simon, B. *The Search for Enlightenment* (Lawrence and Wishart, London, 1990)

[12] *The Burning Question of Education op cit* p.4

[13] McCord, N. *North East England: The Region's Development 1760–1960* (Batsford Academic, London, 1979) p.193

[14] Lawson, J. quoted in *The Right to Learn: The WEA in the North East of England 1910–2010* (WEA, London, 2010) p.7

[15] *ibid* p.7

[16] *The Burning Question of Education op cit* p.22

[17] Walker G., Harvey, G. *The Conflict between the ideology of Industrial Unionism and the practice of its principles in the Durham Coalfield prior to 1914* (Ruskin College, Diploma thesis, 1982) I am unsure if this important piece of research has survived the recent destruction of the Ruskin archives, but, thankfully, there is a copy in Gateshead public library. See also Harvey, G. 'Industrial Unionism and the Mining Industry'. In *Democracy In the Mines* edited by Coates, K. *Documents in Socialist History* (Spokesman Books, Nottingham, 1974) pp.34–35

23

[18] *ibid* pp.34–35

[19] Douglass, D. *George Harvey: Pitmen Bolshevik.* (Follonsby Miners Lodge Banners Association, 2011) p.7

[20] I am grateful to Dr Don Watson and Dave Tate of the North East Labour History Society for this information. There is a pressing need for more research on the history of Robert Blatchford and the *Clarion.*

[21] Walker *op cit* p.24

[22] *ibid* p.25

[23] *What Is Independent Working Class Education?* (The Plebs League, London, 1921) p.7

[24] *Plebs* Vol 1 No 1 February 1909 p.3. There is a very strong possibility that this paragraph was written by Noah Ablett although there is no way of proving its authorship. It has a strong echo of his days as a boy preacher in the Rhondda, especially the references to the tinkling cymbal and sounding brass which is from the 1st book of Corinthians.

[25] *Plebs* May 1915 p.94

[26] *ibid* No 6, July 1914. p.138

[27] Mates, L. *Will Lawther from Revolutionary to Reactionary* (University of Newcastle M.A. thesis, 1996) p.4

[28] Mates *ibid* pp.13–14

[29] Holton, B. *British Syndicalism: Myths and Realities* (Pluto Press, London, 1976) p.112

[30] Ebby Edwards was one of the leading activists for the Plebs League/IWCE in the North East of England. *Plebs* of May 1915 records that Edwards had been lecturing for free in the Ashington area for the previous two sessions. See footnote 25. I discuss Ebby's contribution in greater depth in Chapter 5 of this book.

[31] Lawther W. "An Open Letter to a Durham Miner" *Plebs* December 1916 pp.246–247

[32] See for example the correspondence in *Plebs* between Ebby Edwards of the North Eastern Labour College and James Mactavish of the WEA. *Plebs* April 1917, p.93 and Ebby's long reply *Plebs* Vol 6 1917 pp.127–130.

[33] *North Eastern Labour College Annual Report,* 1925. Page and date of publication not stated. Authors are given as Will Lawther, Will Pearson, James Stewart and Will Coxon.

24

CHAPTER 1
COALING THE EMPIRE
THE NORTHUMBERLAND
AND DURHAM COALFIELD

In the industrial history of the British Isles the Northumberland and Durham coalfield has always had a unique place. This coalfield and the industries that it helped to sustain — shipbuilding, heavy engineering, chemicals, railways, glass making — became part of the nation's folklore. Its exports, both human and material helped not only shape, but also in many cases define the modern world. The names of George Stephenson, Robert Stephenson, William Hedley, Swan Hunter, Vickers-Armstrongs, Joseph Cowen, the Turbinia, the High Level Bridge, Joseph Swan and Cragside became world famous.

This coalfield, which ran, roughly, from Ashington in the north of Northumberland, south into County Durham and west into the prosperous heartlands of the Tyne valley, was long regarded by governments as an iconic part of the nation's industrial fabric. It was there, in the tight knit working class communities of Wallsend, Walker, Jarrow, Hebburn and the mining villages of Durham such as Easington and Chopwell, that the industrial might of the British Empire was formed.

The society that grew out of this combination of factors was one shaped not only by the geology and geography of the region, but also by successive waves of immigration, Celts, Scots, Picts, Romans, Vikings, Jews and, in the middle half of the 19th century, large waves of Irish immigrants seeking a better life and regular work in the fast expanding colliery towns of Northumberland, Durham and Tyneside.

GEOLOGY, GEOGRAPHY AND TOPOGRAPHY

The Northumberland and Durham coalfield had been formed some 295 million years ago during the Carboniferous period which also formed the Whin Sill on which Hadrian's Wall is built. As a result of this development the coal seams in West Durham came up against the Pennines, while in East Durham the seams often overlapped with each other. In Northumberland the coal seams often extended to the coast and out into the North Sea.[1]

Writing in 1915 Stanley Jevons suggested the total size of the Northumberland and Durham coalfield was around sixty miles in length from north to south and between five and thirty miles wide. He writes:

> "It is roughly speaking of triangular form, the apex being on the sea coast near the mouth of the river Coquet. The area of the visible coalfield is about 590 square miles, that of the part overspread by Permian rocks 125 square miles while the area beneath the sea is roughly estimated at 136 square miles. The Northumberland and Durham Coalfield is a trough. About 25 out of 60 known seams are capable of being worked." [2]

At the time Jevons was writing, the Northumberland and Durham Coalfield had been worked for centuries and as he points out "A greater proportion of its resources had already been exploited than is the case in other coalfields, the production was greater than that of any coalfield save for Yorkshire which covered a much larger area." Some figures may help to illustrate this. In 1913 the total amount of coal shipped through the port of Blyth was

3,399,450 tons; Newcastle's figures were 6,418,067, South Shields 5,292,077.[3]

The following table shows the total coal output of the Northumberland and Durham coalfield between 1870 and 1914. The first two columns are coal output. The figures from 1895 onwards show the total number of people employed in the mining industry between those dates.

| | Total coal output | | |
	Durham	Northumber-land	No. of persons employed
1870	21,773,275	5,840,264	
1880	28,063346	6,850,162	
1890	30,265241	9,446,032	
1895	31,133,253	8,694,521	135,627
1900	34,800,719	11,514,521	152,553
1905	37,397,176	12,693,885	159,942
1910	39,431,598	13,121,691	212,350
1911	41,718,916	14,682,427	216,733
1912	37,890,404	13,381,641	218,937
1913	41,532,980	14,819,284	226,817

IMMIGRATION

This phenomenal growth in coal output and employment was conditional on two factors coming together though neither could have happened without widespread and sustained immigration. Beginning in the mid-ninteenth century, large numbers of Irish men and women began crossing the Irish sea, driven not only by destitution after the famine of 1845, but also by the prospect of regular work and the need to escape religious persecution, many of the immigrants being of the Catholic faith.

The need for immigration had been driven by hunger and economic necessity. The Potato Famine drove millions of men and women from their homes; many emigrated to the US to New Zealand and Australia. Those who came to the UK settled in Liverpool, Glasgow and increasingly in the North East where they found work in the chemical, shipbuilding, coal mining and engineering industries.[5]

As John Sheen writes:

> "The immigration of the Irish into the NE brought far reaching consequences for the development of the area. Many monuments bear witness to the labour provided by the Irish. Railway viaducts at Durham and Chester le Street were built by navvies and yet today the industries and the culture that they created have long gone."[6]

Also central to the growth of industry in the North East were large waves of immigration from Scotland. Following on from the Highland Clearances, large numbers of Scots, like their counterparts from Ireland, came south in search of work. So what sort of work did they find and what sort of environment did they endure? W. Richardson perhaps puts it best.

> "Everywhere from the dancing waters of the harbour to the ebb and flow of the throbbing city, industry, resource and expansion, coal staiths, shipyards, engine shops, dry docks, chemical works, forges, electric lighting laboratories, warehouses, at merchants' offices, steamships, railway trains without end, without number — from Shields to Scotswood, there is not its like in 13 miles of river the world over, smoke ridden, grimy, noisy as it all is, what is it but the free expression of nineteenth century energy, the epitome of modern industrialism, the thumb mark of toil by which the human race is destined to work out its salvation?"[7]

By the end of the nineteenth century, Northumberland and Durham, along with South Wales, was one of the largest and best known centres of industry in the world. It was a society where labour was freely available and where a unique combination of factors had come together in a short space of time. As S. Middlebrook suggests:

> "All these interconnected developments, the invention of the steamship and the railway, the tapping of deeper coal

seams, the discovery of Cleveland iron, the building of docks on the Durham coast, the establishment of an effective commission for improving the Tyne and the almost simultaneous foundation of Armstrong's and Palmers, set the stage for the swiftest and most remarkable period of industrial expansion in the whole history of the Northern coalfield."[8]

This phenomenal expansion ran parallel with the growth of an emerging working class consciousness, among the people of Tyneside in the last few decades of the century. In an era where the Liberal party under the leadership of W.E. Gladstone was still dominant, many people looked to the Liberals to solve the country's problems, and the Northumberland and Durham miners were no different, having elected Thomas Burt, a Liberal, to lead the Northumberland Miners in 1874.

When it became clear that that Liberals were incapable of dealing with the region's problems, the working class of Tyneside and Durham began to look for alternatives. They found it in a form of collectivism which stressed community; co-operation and a belief that an injury to one was an injury to all, for increasingly the Tyne and its associated industries were beginning to suffer from overcapacity and unwillingness to invest in new plant and machinery.

If the nineteenth century had given Newcastle its richest and most exciting years, the first two decades of the next would find the Tyne in one of its periodical slumps. Victorian prosperity had caused a phenomenal growth in population from 80,000 in 1851 to 270,000 by 1914.

The problem was that much of this fast expanding labour force was employed in the staple industries of coal, shipbuilding and heavy engineering. The age of the small craftsperson had passed. Now firms felt compelled to expand, to go for bigger products, so that when a national slump occurred, the Tyne suffered more than most. The region's industrial strengths were huge, but there were too few industries to go round. WWI helped to stem the industrial decline, but eventually lead to its collapse. After 1918, the previously safe British markets abroad were never regained.[9]

Nonetheless it remains the case that between 1914 and 1918 there was a massive growth in trade union membership. The Amalgamated Society of Engineers (ASE) grew by more than 117% between 1914 and 1918 and its total funds increased to £2,633,000. Likewise the Boilermakers' Union increased its membership to more than 100,000 by 1919, a gain of almost 50% from 1914, while the shipwrights added 71% over the same period. The six Tyneside branches of the ASE increased their membership by some 12% in 1915. This includes, for example, the Hebburn branch which added 30% and North Shields which gained almost 20%.[10]

Such a massive concentration of industrial and political muscle was sooner or later going to come into conflict with the prevailing economic orthodoxy as personified by the famous Victorian capitalists such as William Armstrong and others, for if the founders of the Independent Working Class Education movement were right, a final reckoning between the forces of Labour and Capital was inevitable. Will Lawther, writing in 1910, perhaps summed it up best.

"The next great step for the workers is to organise educationally. If we as workers are to perform our duties in the political and industrial fields, we must have a clear and definite knowledge of our relations to other classes in society. We must know what position we occupy as workers to our employers. We must not only know who our political opponents are but why they are in opposition. The Central Labour College is an institution which has those objects in view".[11]

So it was that the CLC and the Plebs League were charged with educating the working class, for the great battles that lay ahead, for in this situation there could only be one winner. The Plebs League activists were, though, up against much more than the capitalist class. They were also up against the vision of workers' education being provided by the WEA, and in this philosophy they were to find a formidable opponent, which had the backing of much of the political and educational establishment of the day. This was particularly acute in the North East where the traditions of liberalism allied to the Ruskin College/WEA philosophy had very deep roots. How that hegemony was challenged and what form it took will be discussed later in this book. In the next chapter we will look at the politics of the Northumberland and Durham coalfield in the years just prior to 1914.

FOOTNOTES

[1] Jevons, S. *The British Coal Trade* (Keegan, Paul, Trench, Trubner, London, 1915) p.60

[2] *ibid* p.60

[3] *ibid* p.61

[4] *ibid* p.62

[5] Sheen, J. *Tyneside Irish: A History of the Tyneside Irish Brigade raised in the North East in World War One* (Pen and Sword Books Ltd., Barnsley, 1998) p.9

[6] *ibid* pp.11-12

[7] Richardson, W. 'History of the Parish of Wallsend 1923' quoted in Atkinson, F. *Industrial Archaeology of North East England Vol 1* (David and Charles, Vermont, USA, 1974) p.15

[8] *ibid* p.16

[9] Clark, J. 'Labour in World War One: Some Experiences in Engineering and Shipbuilding on the North East Coast 1914-1918' Quoted in *North East Society of Labour History Bulletin no 12.* (1980, place of publication not stated) p.19

[10] *ibid* p.19

[11] Lawther, W. Quoted in *Blaydon Courier* April 16, 1910 p.3 I am grateful to Mr. Kevin Davies for this information.

CHAPTER TWO
GEORDIE'S LANG MARCH
WORKING CLASS POLITICS
ON TYNESIDE 1900–1914

I stood in Wallsend Shipyard
And looked across the Tyne
The River of my homeland
More famous than the Rhine[1]

The extent to which the Liberal Party was in terminal decline by the beginning of the twentieth century has always been a difficult subject to judge. The retirement of Gladstone in 1894 and his death some four years later marked not only the end of an era, but also the beginning of the end of the long period of Liberal hegemony which had seen Gladstone, the so-called People's William, become Prime Minister on four separate occasions between 1868 and 1894.

Equally difficult to evaluate is the emergence of the Labour Party in those years and to what extent it was a socialist party worthy of the name. A.W. Purdue argued that the North East remained profoundly Liberal in its sympathies.[2] This is probably an accurate reflection of the region's political allegiances in the first decade of the twentieth century, reflected in the fact that both the

Northumberland Miners' Association and the Durham Miners' Association (DMA) were led by Liberals, Thomas Burt and John Wilson respectively.

Joe Batey, later to play a prominent role in the formation of South Shields Labour Party, probably summed up the feelings of many people when he declared "That they had to support the Liberals for they had given workingmen the vote. To vote for any other would be base ingratitude."[3]

Unlike the South Wales coalfield where industrial relations were extremely poor, on account of the difficult geological conditions of coal extraction, the Northumberland and Durham Coalfield was a relatively harmonious region. There does not seem to have been the widespread antagonism between coal owners and employers that was so characteristic of areas such as the Rhondda and yet the difficulties of mining coal were all too apparent regardless of region or locality. The Northumberland and Durham miners would doubtless have recognised the following passage:

> "The hewer down in the mine, away from the sunlight and fresh air, sometimes in a temperature of up to 90°C, every movement of the day inhaling coal and shale dust, perspiring so abnormally (unusually as few men in other industries can realise), head throbbing with the almost inhuman exertion (effort), the roof perhaps 18 inches low, perhaps 20 feet high, ears constantly strained for movements in the strata on which his limbs or his life is dependent, breathing always noxious (harmful smells) due to the absence of any kind of sanitation and to gasses... subject at any moment to the terrible list of mining diseases, most common of which is the dreaded nystagmus, which if neglected may lead to insanity. Liable always to wounds and death from falls of roof... And ever and over all the sickening dread of the awful explosion."[4]

It is within this context of what was at times a brutal struggle for survival as evidenced by the long list of mining disasters about which Roy Thompson has written with such clarity,[5] that we can began to see the beginnings of a labour movement in the North East and the resulting eclipse of the Liberal Party as an electoral force both in the region and at a national level, for what labour and socialist representatives articulated was much closer to the realities of working life for millions of people, than the Liberals could ever have envisaged.

Socialists had been active since the late 1880s among Tynesiders. William Morris was in the area during 1887 promoting his brand of socialism, and the rise of the socialist movement was given added impetus in December 1891 with the launch of the *Clarion* under the guidance of the ex-solider Robert Blatchford.

It is undeniable that the *Clarion* was one of the major reasons for the growth of socialist ideas in the last half of the nineteenth century. Its impact on a generation of labour movement activists cannot be underestimated. As Noah Ablett observed much of his early education was built upon reading Blatchford and Marx.[6] It is fair to assume that there were many North East labour activists who could say the same.

I would suggest that the growth of a socialist movement at both a national and local level was predicated on there being a constant supply of cheap, readily available books. This development was noticeable in the region which had long had a notable autodiact tradition stretching back to self-taught autodidacts such as Chester Armstrong and others.[7]

Running parallel to the growth of a rapidly expanding socialist-labour press was a belief amongst many, on what we would now refer to as the left, that some form of organised labour representation in Parliament was needed to counter the increasing successful attacks of the employing class. The need for such a body had been vividly demonstrated by the Taff Vale Judgement of 1901 which made unions liable for the cost of any labour dispute and demonstrated if proof were ever needed that in an industrial dispute, the courts would always back the capitalist class.

The Labour Representation Committee which grew out of this development was the latest in a long line of attempts to establish labour representation in Parliament, although the ideas of what we would now call socialism had been around for many hundreds of years, both in practical and theoretical form, stretching back to John Ball and the Lollards in the mid-fourteenth century. [8]

The modern expression of labour can be said to have begun with the Labour Representation League of 1869. Both this body and its successor, the Labour Electoral Association, had long been absorbed into the Liberal mainstream and it was not until the formation of the Labour Representation Committee or LRC in February 1900 that any further progress was made.

By the beginning of the twentieth century, bolstered by the formation of the LRC, there was a growing clamour for a socialist party which could best represent the interests of working people. It is within this context that we must see the LRC conference at Newcastle in February 1903 as a watershed in the region's move away from liberalism and towards the idea of socialism which had first seen Keir Hardie elected to Parliament in 1892 as the member for West Ham.

This conference which took place over three days, beginning on the 19th of February, demonstrated the extent to which the labour movement was being pulled in different directions and foreshadowed the deep divisions which were to occur in the period after the first world war, culminating in Black Friday and the General Strike. The chairman's remarks seem in hindsight to be prophetic:

> "Something like a crisis has arisen in the affairs of British trade unionism and the decisions to be given on some of the points in our agenda can hardly fail to affect seriously, perhaps vitally the fortunes and policy of the British Labour Movement in the years to come. Newcastle is somewhat notorious in the matter of policies and programme, particularly programmes. We are met however I take it, not so much to formulate a programme as to consider how we can best carry a given programme into effect."[9]

In these remarks can be seen the pressing need to develop a strategy which would distinguish the LRC from the Liberals. Pete Curran perhaps summed up best the feeling of the conference when he declared:

> "Members of the Executive Committee and affiliated organisations should strictly abstain from identifying themselves with or promoting the interests of any section of the Liberal and Conservative parties in as much as if we are to secure the social and economic requirements of the industrial classes, Labour representatives and out of parliament will have to shape their own policy and act upon it regardless of other sections in the political world, and that the Executive Committee report to the affiliated societies or bodies any such official acting contrary to the spirit of the constitution as hereby amended."[10]

So the gauntlet was thrown down to the Liberal establishment. In many ways the debate was just beginning. The questions which the conference had grappled with were not ones which demanded easy answers, but out of this conference grew a conviction that Labour must have its own independent political party. Keir Hardie articulated the views of many in the hall when he said: "The conference in Newcastle removed all doubt as to what Labour representation meant. It would have its own policy, its own party, its own principles and it would go its own way. It begged no favours from anybody. It would give no quarter to its enemies."[11]

What of those who rejected the parliamentary line entirely and sought emancipation *outside* of parliament, such as George Harvey? In a letter written to the *Newcastle Daily Chronicle* in 1911 Harvey outlined his differences with those who sought emancipation through the parliamentary road:

> "We cannot run the capitalist system of Britain on sentiment. That way is impossible, and if the newer leaders don't know it, the sooner they do the better. We need no tinkering from parliament to better our conditions. The

betterment of these people depends not on a so called
Labour Party, but on the workers themselves. We need
no Moses to deliver us. We must save ourselves.
Therefore let patent medicines go by the board."[12]

So the divide was laid bare. Socialism in the eyes of Harvey,
Ablett and others was not to be achieved by tinkering
through parliament, but by the workers themselves. In
order for that to happen the workers had to have an education which showed not only the fallacies of the capitalist
system, but also the alternative. That alternative was independent working class education (IWCE) and in the
remainder of the book we will examine how that theory
played out in practice among the working people of the
North East, but first it is necessary to discuss briefly what
constituted education in the region for working people in
the early years of the twentieth century.

FOOTNOTES

[1] Davitt, J. *Shipyard Muddling and more Ripyard Cuddling.*
     The Poems of Tyneside Shipyard Worker Jack Davitt (North
     Tyneside Libraries, North Shields, 1993) p.30
[2] Barrow, T. 'The Labour Representation Committee Confer-
     ence at Newcastle Upon Tyne 1903' in *Working Class Politics
     in NE England* ed. Callcott, M. and Challinor, R. (Newcastle
     Polytechnic, 1983) p.38
[3] Clark, D. *We Do Not Want the Earth: The History of South
     Shields Labour Party* (Bewick Press, Whitley Bay, 1992) p.11
[4] Ablett N., Snowden, E., Thomas, J.H., Williams, R., Mann,
     T., Bromley, J. *What We Want and Why* (W Collins, Sons and
     Co., London, 1922) p.142
[5] Thompson, R. *Thunder Underground. Northumberland Mine
     Disasters 1815-1865* (Landmark Publishing, Ashbourne Hall,
     Ashbourne, Derbyshire, 2004) esp. Chapter 2 'The Mining
     Disasters' pp.64-103. As well as the long history of mining
     disasters which included West Stanley in 1910, the shipyards
     were equally as dangerous. My own grandfather lost a leg in
     a shipyard accident in the 1930s while working at Swan
     Hunters for which he received the sum of £500 in compensa-
     tion.

[6] Ablett *op cit* p.139

[7] See for example Chester Armstrong's autobiography *Pilgrimage from Nenthead*. I am very grateful to Dr Jane Platt for the information regarding Chester Armstrong. See also Rose, J. *The Intellectual Life of the British Working Class* (Yale University Press, New Haven and London, 2001) esp. Chapter 2 'Mutual Improvement' pp.58-83 and especially pp.73-75 where Rose discusses the impact of non-conformity on Armstrong's intellectual development.

[8] See for example *Writings on the Wall. A Radical and Socialist Anthology 1215-1984* ed. Benn, T. (Faber and Faber, London, 1984). John Ball's comment as he spoke to the people on the occasion of the Peasant's Revolt is worth recalling "When Adam dalf and Eve span, wo was thane a gentilman" p.228

[9] Barrow *op cit* p.41

[10] *ibid* p.43

[11] *ibid* p.44

[12] Harvey, G. 'Plain Talk to Miners' *Newcastle Daily Chronicle* Thursday November 23 1911 p.8

CENTRAL LABOUR COLLEGE OXFORD.
FRONT VIEW ABOVE.
REAR VIEW, BELOW.

CLASSES & SUBJECTS.

Winter Session 1924–1925.

Where Class is Held.	Subject.	Day & Time.	Secretary's Address.
Ashington Miners' Hut ...	Industrial History, Economics, Philosophy	Thursdays, 7.30 p.m.	*F Millican, 28 Ninth Row.* ~~R. G. Allen, 30, Hawthorn Road,~~ Ashington.
Marsden Miners' Hall, Imeary Street, South Shields ...	Industrial History and Economics	Sundays, 3.0 p.m.	*A Stephenson, 2 Haddock S.* ~~C. Burns, 10, Hartington Terrace,~~ South Shields.
Pelaw Institute, Pelaw-on-Tyne	Short Series of Lectures ...	Wednesdays, 7.30 p.m.	J. Taylor, 8, First Street, Wardley, Co. Durham.
Annfield Plain	Economics		T. Hall, 23, North Terrace, Oxhill, Stanley, S.O.
Chopwell, Blaydon Store Hall ...	Economics ...	Tuesdays, 7.30 p.m.	G. Short, Humber Street, Chopwell, Co. Durham.
Spen	Trade Unionism	Tuesdays, 7 p.m.	J. Curry, 6, Front Street, Spen, Co. Durham
Highfield Council Schools	Imperialism ...	Tuesdays, 6.45 p.m.	J. Newton, 11, Albert Street, Victoria Garesfield, Rowlands Gill, Co.Durham
Rowlands Gill Store Hall	The Co-operative Movement	Tuesdays, 6.30 p.m.	H. Walton, 27, Derwent View, Rowlands Gill, Co. Durham.
Chopwell Store Hall ...	Elementary Class	Mondays, 7.30 p.m.	H. Poskett, Wear Street, Chopwell, Co. Durham.
High Spen Store Hall ...	Elementary Class	Mondays, 7.30 p.m.	J Curry, 6, Front Street, High Spen, Co. Durham.
Newcastle Labour Rooms, Shields Rd., Newcastle-on-Tyne	Economics ...	Sundays, 11 a.m.	S. Evans, 30, Cresswell Street, Byker, Newcastle-on-Tyne.
Newcastle Socialist Rooms	Short Series of Lectures ...	Thursdays, 7.30 p.m.	*F Mawson, 9 Haymarket Bldgs.* ~~J. Davison, 42, Hotspur Street, Heaton,~~ Newcastle-on Tyne.
Scotswood Cafe, Scotswood Road, Newcastle-on-Tyne	Industrial History and Economics	Tuesdays, 7.30 p.m.	A. Turner, 75, Roberts Street, Scotswood, Newcastle-on-Tyne.
Jarrow Labour Rooms, Ellison Street, Jarrow ...	Short Series of Lectures ...	Tuesdays, 7.30 p.m.	*S. Naylor, 18 James St* ~~R. Kane, 70, Monkton Road,~~ Jarrow-on-Tyne.
Fatfield, Birtley Store Hall	Short Series of Lectures ...	Thursdays, 7.30 p.m.	W. Crozier, 9, Short Row, Fatfield, Nr. Washington.
Sacriston Welfare Hall ...	History of Trade Unionism	Wednesdays, 7.30 p.m.	J. Oughton, Eliza Street, Sacriston, Co. Durham.
Sunderland Trade Union Club, Frederick Street, Sunderland ...	Economics ...	Sundays, 11 p.m.	J. Lenagh, 1, Burn Ter., Sunderland.
Do. do.	Speakers' Class	Wednesdays, 7.30 p.m.	Do. do.
Walker Labour Party Rooms ...	Economics ...	Wednesdays, 7.30 p.m.	A. Watson, 657, Welbeck Road, Walker-on-Tyne.
Hamsterley Co-operative Hall, Westwood	Industrial History	Wednesdays, 7 p.m.	R. Farbridge, Jubilee Terrace, Hamsterley Colliery, Co. Durham.
Consett I.L.P. Rooms ...	Industrial History	Sundays,	R. Stoddart, 24, East View, Templetown, Nr. Consett, Co. Durham.

NE LABOUR COLLEGE: CLASSES AND SUBJECTS – 1925. SHEET 1.

Blyth Labour Party Rooms	... Short Series of Lectures ...	Mondays, 7.30 p.m.	J. Kennedy, 28, Dale Street, North Blyth.
Cambois Mechanics' Hall	... Short Series of Lectures ...	Wednesdays, 7 p.m.	J. Lavender, 9, Boat-House Terrace, Cambois, Nr. Blyth.
Birtley Co-operative Hall	... Short Series of Lectures ...	Thursdays, 7.30 p.m.	J. W. Pegg, B.32.t. Elizabethville, Birtley, Co. Durham.
Pegswood, The Club ...	... Economics ...	Tuesdays, 7.30 p.m.	R. Wilson, 4, Block 30, Council Houses, Pegswood, Nr. Morpeth.
Wallsend Assembly Rooms	... Short Series of Lectures ...	Sundays, 11 a.m.	... G. Lamb, 16, Leslie Gardens, Wallsend.
Seaton Burn Co-op. Hall	... Economics ...	Mondays, 7.30 p.m.	J. Whiteside, 7, High Cross Row, Seaton Burn, Dudley, R.S.O.
Lemington Adult Schools	... Short Series of Lectures ...	Mondays, 7 p.m.	P. Carr, 10, Wood Row, Denton Burn, Scotswood. ~~½ Back~~ _Kettle~~nor~~_
Kimblesworth Miners' Hall, Plawsworth Gate	Short Series of Lectures ...	Wednesdays, 7 p.m.	D. Gillespie, ~~16, Lund Avenue, Fram-wellgate Moor,~~ Nr. Durham.
North Shields Labour Rooms, Camden Street	Economic Geography and History of Trade Unionism ...	Tuesdays, 7 p.m.	_F WILLS, 37, HYLTON ST._ ~~H. Braun, 65, Kitchener Terrace,~~ North Shields.
Newsham ...	... History of Trade Union Economics ...	Wednesdays,	J. A. Bell, 2, Beatrice Avenue, New Delaval, Newsham, Nr. Blyth.
Gateshead Bensham Settlement Bensham Road	Eeconomic Geography	Wednesdays, 7.30 p.m.	_M. CONWAY 6. MONK ST_ ~~A. C. Mills, 3, Romulus Street,~~ Gateshead.
Portobello, The Institute	... Industrial History	... Fridays	... T. Law, c/o A. Kay, 60, Castle Street, Fatfield, C. Durham.
Medomsley. Derwent Cottages	Industrial History	... Wednesdays,	J. Wilkinson, Derwent Cottages, Medomsley.
Wallsend Assembly Rooms	... Trade Unionism	... Sundays, 3 p.m.	A. Arridar, 40, Back Buddle Street, Wallsend.
Wallsend Co-operative Hall (Women's Class)	Industrial History	... Mondays, 2.30 p.m.	Mrs. Phillips, 56, George Road, Wallsend
Felling	... Trade Unionism	... Thursdays, 1 p.m.	... ~~H. Patterson, 90, Tulu Street, Felling.~~
New Herrington Miners' Hall, Philadelphia		Mondays, 7 p.m.	J. Lannigan, 22, Best View, Shiney Row, Co. Durham.
Newbiggin-by-the-Sea		Wednesdays, 7.30 p.m.	J. Adams, 16, Emerson Road, Newbiggin-by-the-Sea.

These Classes are free to all Members of the Amalgamated Union of Building Trade Workers, National Union of Dist. and Allied Workers, Amalgamated Engineering Union, Tailor and Garment Workers, and Sheet and Metal Workers, whilst special arrangements as to National Union of Railwaymen has been made by the District Council of that Union. We ask Secretaries of these Unions to draw their Members' attention to the Classes, and urge upon them the importance of attending. Other students pay a small fee ; Local Secretaries of the Classes or the Secretary of the College will gladly furnish any information required.

Short Series includes lectures on Modern Imperialism, Economic Geography, Political Economy, History of Trade Unionism.

We are also willing to give a single lecture to a Trade Union Branch.

START THE NEW YEAR BY JOINING THE CLASSES.

Castletown. Council Elem. Schools.   _Imperialism_   _Sundays 2.P.m._   _W. L. Rutherford, 7, Barron St N, Sunderland._

North Eastern Labour College

(Affiliated to the National Council of Labour Colleges).

ANNUAL MEETING

will be held in the

Socialist Rooms, Royal Arcade, Pilgrim St., Newcastle

On Saturday, 19th September, 1925, at 2-30 p.m.

Coun. W. Pearson

will give an Address on the

International Educational School at Prague,

(CZECHO-SLOVAKIA).

Saturday, 19th September, 1925, at 6-30 p.m.

A Meeting will be held in the Socialist Rooms to make arrangements for the Winter Session.

A Hearty Invitation is given to all.

ALL TUTORS AND CLASS SECRETARIES SHOULD ATTEND THIS MEETING.

YOUR ORGANISATION

is entitled to send TWO DELEGATES to the ANNUAL MEETING.

Wilde & Flesk, 29, Corporation St., Newcastle.

North Eastern Labour College.

Affiliated to the National Council of Labour Colleges.

Organising Secretary—James Stewart, 7, Plantation Street, Wallsend.

EASTER WEEK-END SCHOOL

APRIL 16th and 17th, 1927,

IN

Burt Hall, Northumberland Road, Newcastle-on-Tyne.

LECTURES.

Saturday, April 16th, at 2-30 p.m. — "The Chinese Situation" ···· Will Coxon.
Chairman: Mrs. E. Lawther.

Sunday, April 17th, at 2-30 p.m. — "The Mining Industry" ··· — Ebby Edwards.
Chairman: Pat. Carr.

Sunday, April 17th, at 6-30 p.m. ···· "The International Situation" — Harold Heslop.
Chairman: Jas. Stephenson.

WILL COXON is well-known as an exponent of Independent Working Class Education.

EBBY EDWARDS, one of the founders of the North Eastern Labour College, and well-known in Northumberland for his active work on behalf of the miners.

HAROLD HESLOP is a student recently returned from the Labour College, London.

Send Your Delegates.

A Fee of 1/- per Delegate will be charged. The Delegates should note that Teas can be provided at a very cheap rate by the Newcastle Socialist Society, Royal Arcade, Pilgrim Street, Newcastle.

North Eastern Labour College.

(*Affiliated to the National Council of Labour Colleges.*)

AN

EDUCATIONAL CONFERENCE

To show the need for **"Independent Working Class Education,"** will be held in the **Gaiety Picture Hall, Nelson Street, Newcastle,** on **Saturday, August 23rd,** at **2.30 p.m.**

Chairman **Will Lawther,** (National Executive of Labour Party , and Prospective Labour Candidate for South Shields.

SPEAKERS:

A. J. COOK, (Secretary Miners' Federation of Great Britain.)

CHARLES FLYNN, Prospective Labour Candidate for Hexham Division. Secretary (National Union of District and Allied Workers.)

EBBY EDWARDS, Agent Northumberland Miners' Association.

WILL COXON, (Member of Executive of National Council of Labour Colleges). and supported by prominent Trade Unionists.

Your Organisation is requested to send Delegates to the Conference.

A Delegation Fee of **1/-** per delegate will be charged.

Please return the attached slip with delegation fee to W. COXON, 5, Byron Street, Newcastle-on-Tyne, and Credential Cards will be forwarded to the Delegates.

Yours fraternally,

WILL COXON, *Secretary.*

Name of Delegates with Address : ....

TOP ROW: J.S. WHITEHEAD, E. EDWARDS, A.W. WILLIAMS, J.B. WILKINSON, W.J. EDWARDS, N. ABLETT (CIRCLED),W.J. SADDLER, C. BROCKMAN, J. EVANS, R. SHOTTON, J. JONES. SECOND ROW: A.M. PALFRAMAN, A. BACON, T.E. GROVES, W.J. HIGGON, H. DUCKWORTH, J. DRIVER, J. WALMSLEY, G.H. DIXON, F. STELL, J. PARKS, T. EVANS. THIRD ROW: W.W. CRAIK, G.F.T. BARRETT, G.W. BROWN, F.E. JONES, A. BERREY, W. STEVENSON, J.H.H. BALLANTYNE, R. STRONACH, W. DAVIES, J. RIGG, G. SIMS.

45

RUSKIN COLLEGE, OXFORD. MEMBERS OF THE DURHAM
MINERS'ASSOCIATION 1908.
BACK ROW: R. SHOTTON, J.A. WILKINSON, G. HARVEY.
FRONT ROW: A. MUSGRAVE, J. LAWSON, G.H. DIXON.

CHAPTER 3
LEFT FOR THE RISING SUN, RIGHT FOR SWAN HUNTER
WORKING CLASS EDUCATION ON TYNESIDE

The North East of England has always had a strong tradition of autodiadcatism or working class independent learning allied to a stubborn radical political streak, stretching back to the time of Thomas Spence at the end of the eighteenth century, and into the mid-nineteenth through the efforts of Joseph Cowen, Robert Lowery and others about which Joan Allen has written very convincingly.

It was a radical heritage which encompassed mass meetings on the Town Moor in 1819, post-Peterloo, quite substantial Chartist agitation through newspapers including the *Northern Liberator*, and the support for national liberation movements in places including Italy and Poland. Closer to home Joan Allen notes that the concealed weapons which were allegedly found on the people massacred at Peterloo may have been manufactured in Winlaton.[1]

Clearly the Tyneside radical tradition covered all aspects of society, because if there is one thing that marks the region out towards the end of the nineteeth century, it is the remarkable proliferation of reading rooms, debating societies, literary societies, circulating libraries and mechanics institutes. These ranged from the well-established Literary and Philosophical Society, formed in 1793, through to the ubiquitous circulating libraries and the later campaign for a public library movement in the city. As a result the IWCE movement in the region found fertile soil on which to develop its doctrines of an education rooted in what Gramsci refers to as organic intellectuals, that is to say an education rooted in the everyday experiences of working men and women, for the groundwork had already been carried out.[2]

It was, however, an uphill struggle for the educational and political establishment both here in the North East (which at this time was a Liberal stronghold) and at a national level realised early on that education in the wrong hands could be a very dangerous weapon. As such they were acutely aware of the importance of controlling what people read and how they read. Lord Curzon's sardonic reflections tell us a lot about attitudes to working class education among those tasked with educating the mass of the population and gives a useful pointer to what was considered important. Curzon said "That the only result of extended education which he had noticed was that improper scribblings appeared nowadays lower down on the walls than they used to."[3]

Prior to the 1870 Education Act state education was a fragmented, rudimentary affair, run by voluntary groups and the church with the intention of preparing children for their place in life. As Aristotle tells us "Nature endeavors to make the bodies of freedmen and slaves different.... Instruction is plainly powerless to turn the mass of men to nobility and goodness."[4]

Over many centuries this doctrine had become more or less accepted with the result that only a small percentage of the population received anything approaching a decent education. This state of affairs could be sustained as long as Britain remained a rural agricultural society, but as the Industrial Revolution gathered pace, some educational reformers and what we would now term progressives began to question the wisdom of shutting the masses out of education. This was particularly important in the case of the public library movement and as Maureen Calcott has shown it became a defining moment in the history of late Victorian–Edwardian Newcastle. She writes of the members of Newcastle Mechanics Institute who had asked to be allowed to present the novels of Walter Scott to the library: "That the committee allowed the gift though with the caveat that it should not open the doors to that loathsome trash which had a manifest tendency to vitiate the minds of youth and to waste much youthful time."[5]

If the twentieth century was the age of mass literacy, then the previous century was a titanic struggle in the long campaign for a popular press. Until the abolition of stamp duty in the 1860s newspapers remained the preserve of the middle class and the well off. It would be towards the end of the century before the cheap popular press became readily accessible to a mass audience and it is this which more than anything contributed to a growing autodidact movement among the people of the region.

Notwithstanding the growing influence of publishers such as Charles Kerr of Chicago who in the early twentieth century made available cheap editions of left-wing books for a mass audience, the importance of a cheap popular press in the North East of England can be summed up as: "The politics of print which served 18th C radicals such as Murray and Spence were mobilized in the 19th C to even better effect, engaging the attention of the literate working classes and hear read by countless more in Tyneside's public houses and reading rooms."[6]

Many people such as the tailor Francis Place also had to contend with the social etiquette of the time. Place recalls a customer's disgust when he realised Place had built up a large library of one thousand volumes.

"He expressed much surprise at the number of books, the fitting up and the library table though there was nothing in the least expensive, but it was all neat and in keeping. His remarks were sarcastic and he was evidently displeased. I waited upon him in a few days when some trifling omission being discovered, he told me he supposed I was thinking more about my books than about his orders."[7]

Clearly it would not do for a working man to have literary interests. Place goes on to say:

"Had these persons being told that I had never read a book, that I was ignorant of everything but my business, that I sotted in a public house, they would not have made the least objection to me. I should have been a fellow beneath them, and they would have patronized me, but to accumulate books and to be supposed to know something of their contents, to seek for friends too among literary and scientific men was putting myself on an equality with themselves... an abominable offence for a tailor."[8]

It is within the mid-Victorian mindset that we can see the emergence of an autodidactic tradition on Tyneside as a space where working people could meet, and where periodicals and journals were freely available. That some form of demand for this provision existed is evidenced by an account from the *Northern Liberator* of April 7 1838. The paper notes that on the previous Saturday a meeting was held in St Nicholas' churchyard by the Newcastle Working Men's Association. The motion under discussion was *What are the best means of uniting the people in order to resist and overturn tyranny*? A Mr Devyr opened the meeting by suggesting that it was difficult to get large groups of men together without acting on them through the medium of their senses. He went on to suggest among other things that a working men's hall be erected in towns across the UK and that also women be invited to contribute. The suggestions were broadly welcomed with the paper noting that it was intended to build a working men's hall which it was felt would be beneficial to the public at large.[9]

That such buildings were necessary is evident by some of the subscription fees being charged for reading rooms which in many cases were beyond the reach of all but a handful of skilled artisans. For example, in 1850 the *Newcastle Chronicle* noted that subscriptions were now due for the Central Exchange News room at the sum of ten shillings and sixpence, a vast sum for the time and which may have contributed in some way to the later demand for a free public library movement open to all regardless of income or age.[10]

But for the orphaned and destitute children of Newcastle upon Tyne, there were always the option of the ragged and industrial school. Some flavour of life in one of these schools can be gleaned from the annual report of 1866.

"From year to year fresh little wanderers, ignorant and neglected have been added to its ranks, but it is surely not too much to believe that some have become centers from which good will proceed in other and widening circles and that a harvest will be gathered to the praise of the good Husbandman who has put into the hearts of his people to gather these poor children from homes of vice and wretchedness into this sheltering fold."[11]

In this statement can be seen the Victorian values of faith, hope and charity as they applied to the education of children, a moral and ethical compass for those thought in need of one. It was an education which was at best rudimentary, and at worse nonexistent. After all as the Hammond's concluded:

"All diversions were regarded as wrong, because it was believed that successful production demanded long hours, a bare life, and a mind without temptation to think, or remember to look before or behind.[11] It was said that of the ruling class that with the new method of specialization, industry could not spare a single hour for the needs of the man who served it. In such a system, education had no place."[12]

If the purpose of education was to prepare children for their role in life, what would happen to those children who once they were adults refused to accept the moral certainties of the age? In any given society, there will always be those who for one reason or another don't seem to fit in, and who will push the boundaries of what is considered sociably and culturally acceptable. One such man in this region was Joseph Cowen.

Joseph Cowen was born in 1829 at Winlaton, the son of a family who had by then joined the ranks of the expanding middle class, his father, who later became Sir Joseph having made his fortune initially though bricks and, as his fortunes increased, purchasing a colliery, a railway line and some land. Joseph Cowen Snr. was later to be elected to the Gateshead Board of Guardians who were tasked with implementing the 1834 Poor Law Amendment Act and until his death in 1873 served as Chairman of the River Tyne Commission.[13]

That the Cowen's were undoubtedly a radical family is not in dispute, his father having lead the Winlaton contingent at the Peterloo demonstration on the Town Moor in 1819 while Cowen's mother Mary Newton was acknowledged as a leader of Female Reformers who had also walked on the Town Moor in the same year.[14]

Such a radical lineage could not do anything but influence the young Cowen and by the 1850s, helped by his father's considerable wealth and contacts, he was acknowledged as one of the leading radical personalities of the age, a man who was on friendly terms with such people as Mazzini and Garibaldi and through his purchase of the *Evening Chronicle* able to articulate his views to an ever-widening Tyneside public.

What was it then that turned Cowen towards the path of educational reform and increasingly towards the working class and their education? It has been suggested that part of the reason lay in his father's paternalistic attitude towards his employers which included giving disabled employees as well as the elderly a weekly pension, accommodation and free fuel.[15]

Of far more fundamental importance was the impact of the Northumberland and Durham Colliery Strike of 1844 which marked a watershed in industrial relations and which more than anything else convinced Tyneside radicals like Cowen and W.E. Adams of the importance of education for the masses. As Cowen told the Winlaton Mechanics Institute in 1850: "I have little hope of any material assistance for reform being derived from higher or aristocratic ranks and I have less of obtaining any help from the so called middle classes."[16]

It was to the emerging working class of Tyneside that Cowen turned his attention. Although never a working man himself, he strongly identified with the cause of working class self-emancipation through education. On his return from university in Edinburgh in 1847 Cowen and one or two others founded what became known as the Winlaton Literary and Mechanics Institute. Its aim was an education which was popular and open to both men and women. The subjects covered were of a social and political nature as well as technical and scientific. The guiding principle was to be that of democracy. As Cowen observed in 1883: "Aristocracy is class rule. Ochlocracy is mob rule. Timeocracy is the rule of the rich, but democracy is people's rule, the rule of all rich and poor, lord and labourer, priest and layman. It draws its strength from its universality and its freedom."[17]

The early years of the Mechanics Institutes prior to the opening of the institute in Winlaton were marked by a narrow range of subjects which taught workers basic skills and nothing more. There was, for example, no policy for admitting women. This was an idea which Cowen and his supporters were determined to change, arguing that women should have full rights of membership and this seems to have been the case in practice. For example it was said at the opening of Blaydon and Stella Mechanics Institute "That every male and female, be

53

they ever so poor shall have a sound and rational education."[18]

For the first time there were no restrictions on what could be discussed, nor was there a ban on controversial works of literature such as Darwin's *Origin of Species*. The world that this opened up for working people can only be imagined for it was a world that had long been closed, or which had been thought unsuitable. By 1848 Winlaton Mechanics Institute had a program of lectures on history, moral philosophy, astronomy, chemistry and natural history.[19]

It was through the efforts of Cowen and others like him that the autodidact movement on Tyneside began to take off after 1850, for here at long last was a means by which working people could gain an education on their own terms. The importance of the Mechanics Institutes cannot be underestimated, both for working men and women of Cowen's generation and for those who succeeded him. I would argue that the notion of Independent Working Class Education began not in 1909 with the Plebs League, but much earlier when, for the first time, working people were being encouraged to think for themselves, rather than being the passive recipients of an education which bore little relevance to their everyday working lives.

It was the Mechanics Institutes and other forms of education such as those already noted, which were considered to be out of the mainstream, which encouraged working men and women to question accepted wisdom, both in a written and verbal form, through a series of lectures from which the later University Extension Movement would draw inspiration, and through a number of discussion groups, which taught people the art of public speaking.

Without the pioneering work of the Mechanics Institutes, it is doubtful if the IWCE movement in the North East would have ever got off the ground. The Institutes provided a philosophical and cultural framework which stressed the importance of independent learning, but within a community of likeminded people many of whom would be employed in similar industries such as mining, ship building or heavy engineering. It was a university of autodiadcatism which offered an alternative to walking right for the Rising Sun Colliery at Battle Hill or down Station Road to Swan Hunter and which the activists who formed the Plebs League had reason to be thankful for.

FOOTNOTES

1   Allen, J. *Joseph Cowen and Popular Radicalism on Tyneside 1829–1900* (Merlin Press, Monmouth, 2007) p.18, see especially Ch.2 'Printing and Preaching, Chartists, Republicans and Reformers' and Ch.3 'Knowledge is Power' for Cowen's championing of the Mechanics Institutes and working class education in general.

2   Gramsci, A. Quoted in *The Antonio Gramsci Reader* edited by Forgacs, D. (Lawrence and Wishart, London, 1999) p.195

3   Curzon quoted in *Learn and Live. The Consumer's View of Adult Education* Williams, W.E. and Heath, A.E. (Methuen, London, 1936) p.5

4   Hodgen, M.T. *Workers' Education in England and the United States* (Keegan, Paul, Trench, Trubner, London, 1925) p.3

5   Calcott, M. 'Libraries for the Working Classes in 19C Newcastle' (*Bulletin for the Study of Labour History*, Newcastle upon Tyne, 2004) p.99

6   Allen *op cit* p.27

7   Place, F. quoted in Rose, J. *The Intellectual Life of the British Working Class* (Yale University Press, New Haven and London, 2001) p.22

8   *ibid* p.22

9   *Northern Liberator* April 7 1838, in Newcastle City Library

10   *Newcastle Courant* Jan 18 1850, in Newcastle City Library

11   *Report of the Girls' Ragged and Industrial School for 1866*. Tract 247 042.4 p.7 Library of the Literary and Philosophical Society, Newcastle upon Tyne.

12   Hammond, J.L. and B. quoted in West, E.G. *Education and the Industrial Revolution* (B.T. Batsford, London, 1975) p.4

13   Allen *op cit* p.22

14   *ibid* p.20

15   *ibid* p.20

[16] Todd, N. *The Militant Democracy: Joseph Cowen and Victorian Radicalism* (Bewick Press, Whitley Bay, 1991) p.31

[17] Cowen, Jane (ed.) *Joseph Cowen's Speeches on the Near Eastern Question: Foreign and Imperial Affairs and on the British Empire* (Newcastle Upon Tyne and London, 1909) p.171

[18] *Gateshead Observer* 29 January 1848. Todd *op cit* p.27

[19] *Newcastle Chronicle* 14 July 1848

CHAPTER FOUR
EDUCATING OUR MASTERS
THE DEVELOPMENT OF INDEPENDENT WORKING CLASS EDUCATION ON TYNESIDE 1908/1926

The development of an IWCE movement in the North East was a long and torturous process which was not helped by the region being a bastion of Liberalism personified by the likes of Joseph Cowen and Robert Spence Watson, whose ideology dominated the Northumberland Miners' Association under its leader Thomas Burt, and Durham where the commanding figure of John Wilson lead Durham Miners' Association (DMA) as mentioned earlier.

The Ruskin College strike can be interpreted then as a straightforward fight between the dying embers of Gladstonian Liberalism with its stress on social harmony and cooperation and a growing and increasingly self-assertive socialist movement which saw the need to educate itself without the help of the state or the traditional university or any form of paternalism.

For those students who became active in the early Plebs League, the experience mirrored the non-conformist environment in which so many of them had been raised. Jim

Griffiths, later to become president of the South Wales Miners' Federation, recalls the first time he heard Noah Ablett speak at a meeting in Swansea:

> "On the platform stood this new figure, this young vision-ary with a new gospel. With a quiet voice and with eyes a glitter with his mission, he proclaimed the need for independence in education. Who would provide that edu-cation? The state? The capitalists? No the workers must provide it for themselves."[1]

So what was this new form of education and how did it differ from the liberal curriculum as was being offered by the WEA and Ruskin at this time? IWCE was about workers equipping themselves with the necessary intel-lectual and cognitive skills so as that they could meet the capitalist class on their own terms for the showdown which was looming. The difficulties within the socialist movement on how this showdown was to happen was articulated by Jack Parks, a Northumberland miner who was at Ruskin at the same time as George Harvey. Parks and Harvey agreed on the treacherous role of the trade union leaders and the need for a militant form of indus-trial unionism, but in Park's view the emancipation of the working class must be carried out through direct action. He thought that parliamentary action was a waste of time and it was this that led him to resign from the ILP in 1910 as he told Ray Challinor "I had got disgusted with Ramsay Macdonald. I was tired of the sham fights in Parliament. They weren't doing anything."[2]

In practice this meant looking at Marx's theory of his-tory and applying the methods of historical materialism to the everyday life of working people in whatever locality, situation or workplace they happened to find themselves, with a view to changing their situation for the better. As Marx and Engels argued in *The German Ideology*: "Philosophers have only interpreted the world, in various ways the point is to change it."[3] In practice this meant no collaboration with the capitalist class, no concessions to their politics, educational institutions or their ideology. It was, in the words of Colin Waugh:

> "A step towards socialism from below, because it was about finding things in workers' experiences which would help them understand underlying forces, rather than simply announcing the law of value from above as the key to everything. They saw the study of industrial history as the best preparation for activists planning to use this approach."[4]

So it was that South Wales, the South Wales Miners' Federation (SWMF) and in particular the Rhondda valley became synonymous with the birth of the IWCE movement. Prominent in this struggle was Noah Ablett.

Ablett was born at Ynys-hir on the 4 October 1883, the son of John and Jane Ablett and the tenth of eleven children. His education, like many a working class child of that era, seems to have been no more than basic and the age of twelve he began work at the Standard Colliery in Ynys-hir where he studied for the excise branch of the Civil Service. A serious pit accident curtailed Ablett's ambitions but he continued working in the mines while gaining a political education in the harsh environment of the South Wales coalfield. A letter written by a young Ablett in 1906 gives a tantalising glimpse into his mindset at this time.

Dear comrade

Please excuse my writing to you at Westminster as I did not know where else to write.
I am anxious to obtain all the information I can concerning the LRC as the struggle for affiliation with that body is very keen in this locality. So I enclose 3 half penny stamps which please send LRC constitution and any other information you think would be of assistance to me at your earliest convenience.
Thanking you in anticipation. I remain yours in the cause.

Noah Ablett[5]

Ablett was a voracious reader, a self-educated man and initially a member of the ILP who read Marx, Engels and many other prominent socialist writers of the era, many of whose writings had been imported into the UK by the radical publisher Charles Kerr of Chicago in the early years of the twentieth century. The influence of Charles Kerr on a generation of militant activists cannot be underestimated nor should the influence of the American Marxist Daniel de Leon whose speaking tour in the UK during 1905 galvanized a generation of socialists.[6]

It was not long before Ablett came to the attention of the SWMF leadership and in 1907 went up to Ruskin College on a correspondence course scholarship and later on a scholarship from the Rhondda No. 1 district of the Fed. It was to prove a turning point in his life and a turning point in the industrial history of the UK and the Labour movement. While at Ruskin Ablett does not seem to have taken very long to make his mark, quickly organising classes in Marxist philosophy and history as an alternative to the WEA liberal curriculum being offered by Ruskin at this time. As a member of Ruskin's Marxian Society, he was suspicious of attempts by Oxford University to help the working class, believing, as did Marx and Engels, that the emancipation of the working class must be carried out by the working class themselves. As *Plebs* confidently proclaimed: "Enter the Plebs, not from above, but from below, not to fight a sham battle among the shadows, by the orders and for the interests of our masters, but to fight a real battle in the full light and with a clear knowledge of the issues before us."[7]

For Ruskin's North East contingent of 1908 such as Jack Parks from Prudhoe, Kit Patterson, Harry Floyd, Will Dent, Jack Bacon, and George Harvey, that battle was already beginning to be fought among the numerous miners' lodges and industrial heartlands of Ashington, Wallsend, Byker, Elswick and others.

Also prominent in that struggle for the IWCE cause was a miner from Chevington named Ebby Edwards.

Ebby Edwards was born in 1884, a year after Noah Ablett, and some five years prior to Will Lawther whose admiration for Ablett has already been documented. In much the same way as his contemporaries his education was basic and he went straight into the pits. Evidence of Ebby's early life is fragmentary, but there is a note of him applying for a Ruskin correspondence scholarship. The letter is dated 24 December 1907 and is signed by Bertram Wilson, General Secretary of Ruskin College to William Straker President of the Northumberland Miners' Association (NMA). It states:

Ebenezer Edwards of 79 Tenth Row Ashington tells me that he is applying for one of the scholarships at Ruskin College established by your Association. He wishes me to tell you of the work he has done for us in the Correspondence School. He joined us in January this year and has taken the following subjects: The Labour Movement and the History of our Times and he has written five essays which have been corrected by us.[8]

Having gone up to Ruskin in 1908 following successful completion of the Ruskin correspondence course, Ebby was forced to leave Ruskin early due to lack of money and to return to Ashington. When his father who was an official of Ashington Lodge resigned, Ebby took his place and this is how he managed to support himself for the next several years. He was extremely lucky as victimisation of what were perceived to be militants was widespread at this time. The *Newcastle Chronicle* of 1911 reported a meeting of the Northumberland Miners' Council at Burt Hall in which the reinstatement of miners who had been to Ruskin was discussed. The resolution was read out on behalf of the Ruskin students which stated "That the students representing numerous trades and nationalities entered its emphatic protest against the actions of the Backworth Colliery owners in refusing work to John Mackay on his return from Oxford".[9] The resolution was carried with a note of exasperation which read "All constitutional

61

methods have exhausted in trying to get a Ruskin College student his work in the district. We now seek a meeting with the owners' association with a view to getting him work in the district to which he belongs."[10]

Given the circumstances described above, what happened to John Mackay was probably not unusual. The only thing we can say with any certainty is that while at Ruskin Ebby Edwards became aware of the simmering discontent among the students and began to advocate Marxism. This is hardly surprising. Ruskin at this time was home to some of the most militant students in the country, men who within a year or two would be leading the Cambrian Combine strike and other industrial disputes which came to define the era. It is inconceivable that Ebby was not influenced by Noah Ablett and the other Welsh militants with whom he would have come into contact. Their influence was to have a lasting impact on his life and career.

On his return home, Edwards began to campaign for IWCE in the area and the first recorded evidence appears in *Plebs* in 1911. This was an analysis of the writings of Joseph Dietzgen whose book *The Positive Outcome of Philosophy* had had such an impact on the autodidacts at Ruskin.

Joseph Dietzgen 1828–1888 was a German philosopher, a friend of both Marx and Engels, who developed Marx's theory of history (the dialectic) in a number of books, the most widely read of which was *The Positive Outcome of Philosophy* published in 1887.

Although his work feels somewhat dated now, Dietzgen's impact on Marxist thinking was such that he was able to reconcile the differences between anarchists and Marxists, a considerable achievement given the enmity and distrust that existed (and still does exist) between different groups on the left. As Dietzgen said. "For my part I lay little stress on the distinction, whether a man is an anarchist or a socialist, because it seems to me that too much weight is attributed to this difference." [11]

Ebby Edwards begins his discussion of Dietzgen by acknowledging this and states that Dietzgen conceived of the world as an invisible whole in which knowledge is a description of parts, qualities and relations.[12] According to Edwards there are no entire realties, no isolated entities. A thing in order to be real must be in relation to something else and that knowledge must be born out of experience in much the same way that Marx and Engels argued. It is, to use a Marxist term, praxis, that is to say the unity between theory and practice that is of primary importance in understanding the world and looking to change it. Edwards went on to suggest that the objective qualities of form and interrelation are imported into the mind by experience. In other words what cannot be seen nor heard or felt has no claim to existence since it cannot be proven. This would deny the role of religious thought and especially the non-conformist radical tradition in which the likes of Ablett, Mark Starr (see below) and others had been raised.[13]

So if Dietzgen, Marx and others were right, knowledge is not an abstract concept. It is born out of the realities of working life allied to class struggle, and through this working people will come to see their interests are opposed to those of the capitalist class. From this will come class war and the overthrow of the bourgeoisie through revolution, leading to a socialist society.

This was the aim of the Plebs League and the reason for its existence, but for that revolution to happen the workers had to be educated beyond the rudimentary level and that meant a course of study. As Charles Kerr observed: "There could be no educated socialists without socialist books. The route to political power lay in the study and application of scientific socialism."[14] And so the Plebs League began to publish its own textbooks for use by the worker students. One of the most famous of these entitled *A Worker Looks at History* by Mark Starr, first published in late 1917.

Mark Starr was born on April 27 1894 in the village of Shoscombe near Bath. He was the second son of William Starr, a coal miner, and his wife Susan. There were three brothers and three sisters in the family. Although the family were staunch non-conformists, the young Mark attended an Anglican primary school, St Julian's in Shoscombe, until he began work in 1907. His father was a leading light in the local Free Methodist chapel and, despite having no formal education, had taught himself to read and write, rising to become superintendent of the Free Methodist Sunday School in the village. Mark followed in his father's footsteps and became a Sunday school teacher before his growing religious scepticism forced him to abandon the chapel.

In later years Starr was to recall that his separation from the chapel did not happen overnight, but was part of a slow process which began with reading Ruskin, Blatchford, Huxley and Marx which caused him to turn towards the materialist conception of history.[15] There were also at the time what we would now term as progressives within Methodism who wanted an active social ministry. They were to come up against a traditional interpretation of the bible which stressed salvation as an individual concept. Starr seems to have come into conflict with the traditionalists when he sought to advance a more enlightened version of the gospel.

Starr's intellectual influences were one thing. The world of work was quite another. Ralph Dumain notes that aged just thirteen Starr took a job as a mortar boy and hod carrier for a local builder earning the princely sum of 4d for fifty-six and a half hour week. Later he went to work in Writhlington pit where the working conditions in the narrow seams were appalling. His first job was a carting boy, a job which involved hauling tubs of coal using the Gus and Crook, a hideous device which chained the child to the coal tubs.[16]

Starr's rejection of religion as a force for social change was compensated by his growing involvement in the labour movement. He was by now a reader of the *Clarion* and an active member of the ILP which was organising meetings for future Labour cabinet members such as Margaret Bondfield.

This period in Starr's life was to prove useful for, in 1912, like many a Somerset miner before him, he made the relatively short trip to the rapidly expanding collieries of South Wales beginning in Mynachdy and subsequently several pits in the Aberdare and Rhondda area. It was while working in the Rhondda that Starr came into contact with the members of the Unofficial Reform Committee who were by this stage some of the most militant class conscious miners in Britain.

It was not the likes of Noah Ablett, however, who would be the formative influence on Starr at this time. That distinction belonged to John Thomas, the first full-time district secretary of the WEA in South Wales. Thomas was at this time running a class in industrial history at Ynysybwl near Pontypridd and, perhaps recognizing Starr's intellectual gifts, had no hesitation in providing a reference for him when in 1915 Mark Starr went up to the Central Labour College on a scholarship provided by the Rhondda No. 1 District of the South Wales Miners Federation. Starr recalled many years later that the CLC had given "Point and purpose to my views of life and furnished me with a guiding thread whereby the complete development of society — that tangled skein can be understood. Light has shone in dark places. Contradictions are understood and reconciled. The new can be seen evolving form the old. The solution is contained in the problem."[17]

On his return from the CLC Starr found himself victimised by the colliery owners as were so many others, and so he began teaching classes in Industrial History. These classes were so popular that they were republished under the title *A Worker Looks at History*, the book mentioned earlier.

This was an immediate success among worker students at a time of massive expansion among the IWCE movement in South Wales. Today it too is considered dated, and too deterministic in its working out of a linear historical process, but needs to be placed in the proper context of the time.

In 1917 in the midst of a war, with a revolution under way in Russia, Starr's book seemed to offer intellectual justification for the socialist cause, a means of understanding the momentous changes that were taking place in the world, and the hope that a new socialist dawn was on the horizon. As Starr puts it:

> "In every country capitalism begets its grave diggers. In its endeavours to increase its profits, it will force the workers to take up a militant attitude upon the industrial, political and educational fields, and progress will be accelerated until the workers of the world will unite and their emancipation be accomplished. To the Day."[18]

In 1918 Mark Starr was called up for the army, but, like many a member of the ILP, refused service on the basis of Conscientious Objection. It was while in prison that he developed a lifelong interest in Esperanto, and following his father's intervention with the Liberal MP Sir John Barlow, Starr was transferred to work on the farms in Northumberland. It was at this point that he became active in the NE Labour College movement and met up with other activists including Ebby Edwards.

On his release from prison Starr returned to the South Wales Coalfield where he managed to obtain a further years scholarship at the CLC. Following this he became one of the first organisers for the newly formed National Council of Labour Colleges which had been formed to unite the various disparate elements of the Labour College movement in the aftermath of WW1.

The formation of the NCLC was something that Starr had been advocating for a long time. Following the end of the war, the original IWCE network had been swelled by thousands of returning ex-servicemen who wanted an education of the type being offered by the WEA and the

CLC and there was a desperate need for some form of organisation and central control. The solution was to be the end of the original ideal of IWCE as it had been conceived in the heady pre-war days of 1908 when anything seemed possible. From now on there would be much more central control over what was taught and how it was taught. Much less emphasis on challenging the prevailing orthodoxy. The years from 1921 onwards saw a process of retrenchment as the revolutionary tide of 1917 ebbed.

While the reorganisation of the IWCE movement was necessary, it is undeniable that something was lost in the process. The fighting spirit and mood of optimism that so characterised the movement pre-1921 was replaced by a much more sober mood as the economic and political realties of the 1920s began to take shape. The final chapter of the book looks at these realties and considers what if anything could have been done differently.

FOOTNOTES

[1] Noah Ablett Obituary *Plebs* 1935 Vol 28 no 12 p.296
[2] Ray Challinor — interview with Jack Parks, 1975. I am grateful to the North East Labour History Society for this information.
[3] Marx, K. & Engels, F. *The German Ideology* Student edition, ed. Arthur., C. (Lawrence and Wishart, London, 1970) p.123
[4] Waugh, C. *Plebs: The Lost Legacy of Independent Working Class Education* (*Post-16 Educator*, Sheffield, 2009) p.14
[5] Ablett, N. Letter is in the People's History Museum, Manchester. Ref LPGC.6/4. Noah Ablett, like many a working class activist of the era, left little personal correspondence. We are lucky to have his articles in *Plebs,* his textbook *Easy Outlines of Economics* and his letters to the local press in South Wales. Sadly, after around 1923, with his increasing dependence on alcohol, his letter writing ceases. The IWCE activists were not to know that one hundred years later, people would be searching for information on them.
[6] See for example Ruff, A. *We Called Each Other Comrade: Charles H. Kerr & Company Radical Publishers* (PM Press, Oakland, California, 2011) esp. Ch. 6 'The First Socialist Phase 1899–1908' pp.83–110. It is argued along with the

influence of the Non-Conformist Movement, Charles Kerr was partially responsible for the growth of IWCE in the UK. Being able to read Marxist and left-wing texts in an easy accessible form and at a sensible price allowed the spread of ideas and debate among a generation of activists previously denied this luxury. See also De Leon, D. *The Socialist Reconstruction of Society* (Socialist Labour Press Edinburgh, the pamphlet is not dated, but the address is given in 1905).

7 *Plebs* Vol 1. No 3 April 1909 pp.41–45

8 Bertram Wilson to William Straker, Secretary of the Northumberland Miners 24 December 1907. Northumberland Archives, Woodhorn. NRO 3793/155. Ebby Edwards left little or no written correspondence. What information exists is taken from his entry on Wikipedia and from the Northumberland Archives at Woodhorn. I am therefore grateful to the North East Labour History Mapping Popular Politics Project for their research, in particular Hillary Love. For information on this important database of North East History, see www.nelh.org.

9 *Newcastle Chronicle* Wednesday November 22 1911 p.8 (in Newcastle City Library)

10 *ibid*

11 Dietzgen, J. Information taken from his Wikipedia entry

12 Edwards, E. 'The Philosophy of Joseph Dietzgen' *Plebs* No 11 p.248 1911

13 *ibid*

14 Ruff, A. *We Called Each Other Comrade*. Charles H Kerr and Company Radical Publishers (PM Press, Oakland, California, 2011) p.99

15 Dumain, R. The Autodidact Project (www.autodidactproject.org) is a little known but deeply rewarding web based archive. There is a considerable amount of information here on Mark Starr and other little known autodidacts.

16 *ibid*

17 *ibid*

18 *ibid*. The Gus and Crook was a truly horrible device which fitted around a child's body like a strap, so they were able to haul coal tubs. I am told that this device was only abolished with the advent of nationalisation in 1948. I am grateful to Dr Richard Lewis and to Dave Chapple for this information especially regarding Mark Starr's arrival in the North East of England. I am told that he was introduced to Will Lawther while in prison as a C.O. and that it was Lawther who managed to get Starr a job on the farms in Northumberland. Like many an activist of this era, including Noah Ablett, Starr needs a decent biography.

CHAPTER 5
A REVOLUTIONARY MOMENT PASSED
RETREAT AND RETRENCHMENT
1921−1926

We have already seen how by the beginning of the 1920s, both the labour movement and that of IWCE were at their zenith. Twelve years of non-stop propaganda and an almost messianic belief in the transforming power of education had given the working class activists of the Plebs League a power and influence they could have only dreamt about a decade earlier, Tommy Jackson, an autodidact and one time IWCE tutor in the NE, recalled that:

> "The war had in fact given a great impetus to the study class movement. It set workers thinking about the causes of things political as they had never thought before, and it was in practice far easier as well as safer to propagate the concept of class struggle and revolution through such classes than it was by the traditional methods of political agitation. This upstirring had been enormously quickened by the event of the Bolshevik revolution and by the consequent struggle against the war of intervention under the slogan of 'Hands off Russia'."[1]

The Russian Revolution of October 1917 provided the IWCE movement with its greatest impetus. For the first time people such as Noah Ablett, Mark Starr, John

Maclean and others could see what a workers' state could look like in practice as opposed to just relying on theoretical discourse. Bill Craik in his history of the CLC recalled that:

> "Everyone at Earls Court was deeply stirred by the Russian Revolution of 1917 and followed with keen interest and sympathy, the successful development immediately following it, leading to a third of the globe being transformed into a land and a people who had turned their backs on capitalism and were shaping for themselves a society in which for the first time, they could become masters of their destiny.
>
> About one third of the students joined the British Communist Party almost as soon as it was formed. Some of their successors were already members of the CP even before they arrived at the college. The Russian Revolution had the effect of augmenting the interest and the keenness of all its students in the study of Marx."[2]

The problem of course was that the capitalist class could also see a workers' state. They looked over the abyss and what they saw terrified them and as a result, they began planning for the aftermath of war, when the problems of dealing with not only mass unemployment, but also a revolutionary situation created by the events of 1917 would have to be faced.

It was around this time that the state began taking an interest in the burgeoning labour college movement with the intention of destroying it as a movement. Some of the sense of fear and apprehension engendered by 1917 is shown in the following report on revolutionary organisations in the UK:

> "James Stewart of 15 Woodbine Avenue Wallsend, a conscientious objector and a member of the Independent Labour Party has opened a shop for the sale of revolutionary literature. He is an agent of the Socialist Labour Press, and he has now opened classes for teaching 'Social, economic and industrial history'. The classes are attended by a few youths of from 18 to 21."

In Derbyshire where nationalisation meetings have been badly attended, revolutionary feeling is rapidly increasing. Many of the miners' agents are extremists and advocates of Bolshevism and their speeches are well received, whereas allusions to Bolshevism were received in silence six months ago. A meeting held by Major Waring at Chopwell was practically broken up by the local miners who sang the Red Flag and cheered Lenin and the Russian Soviet. Their extremist leader is President of the North Eastern Labour College classes."[3]

The realities alluded to at the end of chapter four meant that sooner or later some form of restructuring of the Plebs League would have to take place. It was simply not feasible to continue in the way that the League had previously functioned and already in 1918 there had been talk of organising the movement into seven national divisions.

In November 1919 shortly after the post-war reopening of the CLC, there had been discussions as to how the activities of the Plebs League and the CLC could be better coordinated. Speaking on behalf of the EC, Mark Starr argued for the creation of autonomous braches in which the only stipulation should be an adherence to the philosophy and methods advocated by the Plebs League.

Starr suggested that these branches should arrange classes, encourage the distribution of the *Plebs* magazine and generally stimulate interest in Independent Working Class Education. There should be annual general assembly, which should have only a consultative function, and any constitutional amendments should be effected by a postal vote.[4]

Mark Starr's proposal was put to a meeting of the EC on 17 and 18 Jan 1920 when the decision was ratified to organise the Plebs League into branches, which should be responsible for organising classes and selling books and pamphlets. It was also decided that full time organisers should be appointed with a salary equivalent to that of a skilled worker and given, if need be, proper expenses.

71

Plebs noted "The general feeling was that decentralisation with coordination was the ideal policy, and that neither the Labour college nor the Plebs League regarded a centralised authority as either practical or desirable."[5]

In hindsight this is exactly what happened, and so the question must be asked, how did the IWCE movement, which at the end of WW1 was at its peak, degenerate so rapidly, so that by the time of the General Strike, it was a shadow of its former self? The answers are many and complex, but I would argue that the growing counter offensive of the capitalist class which had resulted in Black Friday, and the divisions which were opening up in the labour movement between right and left meant that the day of reckoning could no longer be postponed. More importantly, did the Labour leaders of the time have the confidence in their own abilities to carry out a Bolshevik style revolution in 1919 and could they, would they have succeeded?

Aneruin (Nye) Bevan, a CLC student from 1919 to 1921, recalled a story he was told by Bob Smillie of the Scottish Miners which graphically illustrates the pressures that the labour movement were facing in the aftermath of World War One. The pressures were not only financial:

> "I remember vividly Robert Smillie describing to me an interview the leaders of the Triple Alliance had with David Lloyd George in 1919. The strategy of the leaders was clear. The miners under Robert Smillie, the transport workers under Robert Williams and the National Union of Railwaymen under J.H. Thomas formed the most formidable combination of industrial workers in the history of Great Britain. They had agreed on the demands that were to be made on the employers, knowing well that the government would be bound to be involved at an early stage and so it happened. A great deal of industry was still under government wartime control and so the state power was immediately implicated."

Lloyd George sent for the Labour leaders and they went truculently, determined that they would not be talked possible to speak of an IWCE movement and if so what would it look like?

Recently a group of activists have sought to establish a modern version of the IWCE movement, but one which takes account of modern ways of organising. As I write the beginnings of what is hoped will be a rejuvenated movement are taking shape.

The impetus of the modern IWCE movement grew out of the success of Colin Waugh's 2009 pamphlet *Plebs: The Lost legacy of Independent Working Class Education* and since then has gone from strength to strength with successful day schools at the Working Class Movement Library in Salford, and the South Wales Miners' Library in Swansea among others.

Details of this orgainsation can be found at IWCEducation.co.uk. There is clearly a need for an education which can challenge the prevailing orthodoxy. The modern IWCE movement has inherited a fantastic and long-established tradition of Independent Working Class Education and it is hoped that this can continue.

The challenge is now to grow and to train the next generation of labour activists, and for that we must have a modern well-equipped and functioning labour college which can provide a platform for discussion and debate. If we can achieve this, then we will have accomplished something of which Noah Ablett would have been proud, and we will have in the words of the great Roman poet Virgil *Nostris, Aliquis, exsobsis Ultor (Arise Avenger from my bone).*

Is the labour movement up to the task and will people rise to the challenge? As the Plebs League would have recognised, this *is* the burning question of education for the twenty-first century and its one that we must face.